# WORLD WAR I

## COMMEMORATING THE
## 100TH ANNIVERSARY

KIM LOCKWOOD

Published by:
Wilkinson Publishing Pty Ltd
ACN 006 042 173
Level 4, 2 Collins St Melbourne, Victoria, Australia 3000
Ph: +61 3 9654 5446
www.wilkinsonpublishing.com.au

International distribution by Pineapple Media Limited
(www.pineapple-media.com)    ISSN 2200 – 7929

National Library of Australia Cataloguing-in-Publication entry
Author:     Lockwood, Kim, 1944- author.
Title:      World War I - 100th anniversary / Kim Lockwood.
ISBN:       9781922178381 (paperback)
Series:     WP military series.
Subjects: World War, 1914-1918.World War, 1914-1918
            --Anniversaries, etc.
Dewey Number: 940.4

Photos and illustrations by agreement with international agencies, photographers and illustrators including Getty Images and Press Association.

Design: Michael Bannenberg
Printed in China.

## THE AUTHOR

Kim Lockwood is an acclaimed author with a keen interest in Australian history. Growing up in Darwin after the war – his father, journalist and author Douglas Lockwood was there for the bombing on 19 February 1942 – he later worked as a journalist in Perth, back in Darwin (where he lived through cyclone Tracy) and Melbourne, undertaking senior editorial roles for the Herald and Weekly Times and News Ltd. He is the author of or contributor to 16 books, including *Charles 'Bud' Tingwell's War Stories*.

Erzherzog Franz Ferdinand von Oesterreich
und Herzogin von Hohenberg.
† Sarajevo, den 28. Juni 1914.

# The spark

Leopold Lojka started World War 1 by taking a wrong turn. It was 28 June 1914, and General Oskar Potiorek, Governor of the Austrian provinces of Bosnia and Herzegovina, had invited Archduke Franz Ferdinand and Countess Sophie to the opening of a hospital. The Archduke knew the visit would be dangerous. His uncle, Emperor Franz Josef, had been the target of assassins in 1911.

Just before 10am, the royal couple arrived in Sarajevo by train. In the front car of their motorcade was the Mayor of Sarajevo, Fehim Čurčić, and the city's Commissioner of Police, Dr Edmund Gerde. Franz Ferdinand and Sophie were in the second car with General Potiorek and Lieutenant Colonel Count Franz von Harrach. The car's top was rolled back to give the crowds a good view of royalty.

Six Bosnian Serb conspirators seeking their region's freedom from Austria-Hungary were spaced out along the Appel Quay, each with instructions to kill Franz Ferdinand. The first to see the royal car was Muhamed Mehmedbašić, but he lost his nerve and

allowed the car to pass. He later said a policeman was standing behind him and feared he would be arrested before he had a chance to throw his bomb.

At 10.15, as the procession passed the central police station, nineteen-year-old Nedeljko Čabrinović hurled a hand grenade at the Archduke's car. The driver accelerated when he saw the object flying towards him, but the grenade had a 10-second delay and exploded under the fourth car. Two occupants were seriously injured. To avoid capture, Čabrinović swallowed a cyanide capsule and jumped into the River Miljacka to make sure he died. The cyanide pill was out of date and made him sick, but failed to kill him, and the river was only 10cm deep. A few seconds later he was hauled out by police.

The four other conspirators could not attack because of the crowds and the speed of the Archduke's car.

Franz Ferdinand later decided to visit the victims of Čabrinović's bombing. To avoid the city centre, General Potiorek

"One day the great European War will come out of some damned foolish thing in the Balkans."

Otto von Bismarck, 1888

decided the royal car should go straight along the Appel Quay to the hospital. But he forgot to tell the driver, Leopold Lojka. On the way, Lojka turned right into Franz Josef Street.

Conspirator Gavrilo Princip was standing near Moritz Schiller's cafe when he saw Franz Ferdinand's car drive past, having taken the wrong turn. But after being told of the mistake, Lojka braked and began to reverse. The engine stalled and the gears locked. Princip stepped forward, drew his pistol (a .380 calibre FN Model 1910), pistol-whipped a pedestrian, and from about 1.5m fired twice into the car. Franz Ferdinand was hit in the neck and Sophie in the abdomen. They both died before 11am.

The assassination triggered a diplomatic crisis when Austria-Hungary delivered an ultimatum to the Kingdom of Serbia. Several alliances were invoked.

Exactly a month later, on 28 July, Austria-Hungary declared war against Serbia and fired the first shots. Within weeks, the major powers were at war, and via their colonies, the conflict soon spread around the world.

"I look upon him as the greatest criminal known for having plunged the world into war."

King George V
on his cousin Kaiser Wilhelm II, 1918

# The growth of Germany

German industrial and economic power grew quickly after the Empire was founded in 1871. From the mid-1890s, the government of Kaiser Wilhelm II spent large sums to build up the Imperial German Navy, established by Admiral Alfred von Tirpitz, in rivalry with the Royal Navy. With the launch of HMS *Dreadnought* in 1906, the British Empire increased its advantage. The arms race between the two countries eventually extended to the rest of Europe, with all major powers producing the equipment and weapons needed for war. Between 1908 and 1913 the military spending of European powers increased 50 per cent.

Austria-Hungary precipitated the Bosnian crisis of 1908–1909 by officially annexing the former Ottoman territory of Bosnia and Herzegovina, which it had occupied since 1878. This angered Serbia and its patron, the Orthodox Russian Empire. Russian manoeuvring destabilised peace accords, which were already cracking in what was known as "the powder keg of Europe".

In 1912 and 1913, the First Balkan War was fought between the Balkan League and the Ottoman Empire. The resulting Treaty of London further shrank the Ottoman Empire, creating an independent Albanian state and enlarging the holdings of Bulgaria, Serbia, Montenegro, and Greece.

After Princip killed Franz Ferdinand, Austria-Hungary, Germany, Russia, France and Britain began a month of diplomatic manoeuvring. Wanting to end Serbian interference in Bosnia, Austria-Hungary delivered 10 demands intentionally made unacceptable, intending to provoke a war. When Serbia agreed to only eight demands, Austria-Hungary declared war on 28 July 1914.

The Russian Empire, unwilling to allow Austria-Hungary to end its influence in the Balkans, ordered a partial mobilisation a day later. The German Empire mobilised on 30 July, ready to apply the Schlieffen Plan, which planned a quick, massive invasion of France to eliminate the French army, then a thrust east against Russia.

The French Cabinet resisted military pressure for immediate mobilisation and ordered its troops to withdraw 10km from the border to avoid any incident. But France mobilised on 2 August when Germany invaded Belgium and attacked French troops. Germany declared war on Russia the same day. Britain declared war on Germany on 4 August after an "unsatisfactory reply" to the British ultimatum that Belgium must be kept neutral.

It was on.

# Opening hostilities

The strategy of the Central Powers – Germany and Austria-Hungary – suffered from miscommunication. Germany had promised to support Austria-Hungary's invasion of Serbia, but interpretations of what this meant differed. Previous plans had been replaced early in 1914, but the replacements had never been tested in exercises. Austro-Hungarian leaders believed Germany would cover its northern flank against Russia, but Germany envisioned Austria-Hungary directing most of its troops against Russia while Germany dealt with France. This confusion forced the Austro-Hungarian Army to divide its forces between the Russian and Serbian fronts.

On 9 September 1914, Germany outlined a plan that detailed its war aims and the conditions it sought to force on the Allied Powers. It was never officially adopted.

# Serbian campaign

Austria invaded Serbia and fought its army at the battles of Cer and Kolubara, starting on 12 August. Over the next fortnight, Austrian attacks were rebuffed with heavy losses, which marked the first Allied victories of the war and ended Austro-Hungarian hopes of a quick victory. This forced Austria to keep forces on the Serbian front, weakening its efforts against Russia.

# Germany in Belgium and France

"The War was decided in the first twenty days of fighting, and all that happened afterwards consisted in battles which, however formidable and devastating, were but desperate and vain appeals against the decision of Fate."

Winston Churchill

At the start of the war the German army carried out a modified version of the Schlieffen Plan. This moved German armies through neutral Belgium and into France before turning south to circle the French army on the German border. The plan was that Germany should not attack through the difficult terrain of Alsace-Lorraine, but try to quickly cut Paris off from the English Channel and British assistance and take Paris, thus winning the war. Then the armies would move east to Russia. Russia was believed to need a long period of mobilisation before they could threaten the Central Powers.

Germany wanted free escort through Belgium to invade France. Neutral Belgium rejected this, so the Germans decided to invade. France also wanted to move their troops into Belgium, but Belgium rejected this "suggestion" as well, hoping to avoid war on its soil. In the end, after the German invasion, Belgium tried to join its army with the French, but a large part of its army retreated to Antwerp, where they were forced to surrender when all hope was gone.

The German plan called for the right flank of their advance to bypass the French armies (which were concentrated on the Franco-German border, leaving the Belgian border without significant French forces) and move south to Paris. Initially the Germans were successful, particularly in the Battle of the Frontiers (14–24 August). By 12 September, the French, with help from the British, halted the

German advance east of Paris at the First Battle of the Marne (5–12 September), and pushed the German forces back 50km. The last days of this battle signalled the end of mobile action in the west and, despite the war being less than two months old, marked a point from which the Central Powers never recovered.

In the east, the Russians invaded with two armies, surprising the Germans, who had not expected an early move. A field army, the 8th, was rapidly moved by rail across the German Empire to East Prussia from its role as reserve for the invasion of France. This army, led by General Paul von Hindenburg, defeated Russia in battles known as the First Battle of Tannenberg (17 August–2 September).

# Western Front

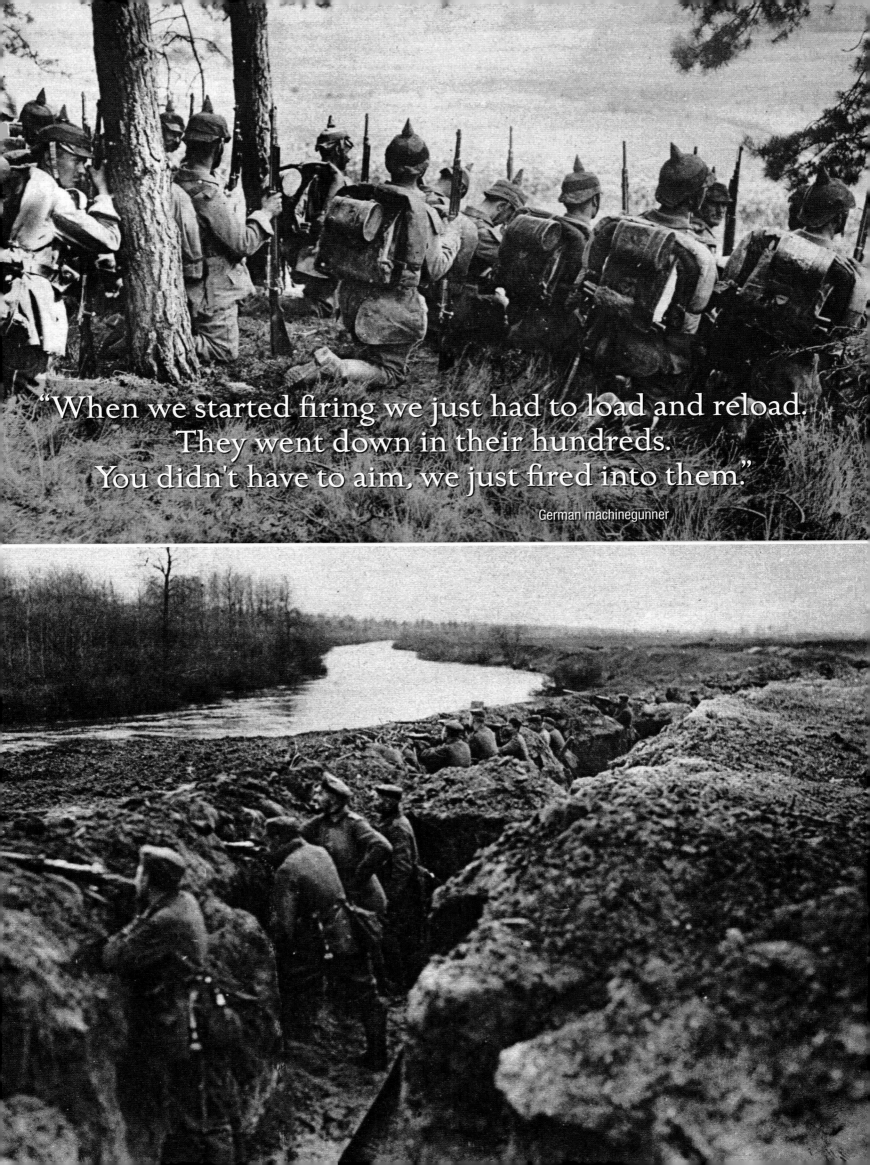

"When we started firing we just had to load and reload.
They went down in their hundreds.
You didn't have to aim, we just fired into them."

German machinegunner

## Trench warfare begins

Military tactics had not kept pace with technological advances, which allowed for defence systems that the out-of-date tactics could not break through for most of the war. Barbed wire was a significant hindrance to massed advances. Artillery, much more lethal than in the 1870s, coupled with machineguns, made crossing open ground hard. Commanders on both sides failed to develop tactics to breach entrenched positions without heavy casualties. In time, however, technology began to produce new offensive weapons, such as gas and the tank.

After the First Battle of the Marne, both Allied and German forces began outflanking manoeuvres in the so-called "Race to the Sea". Britain and France soon faced an uninterrupted line of entrenched German forces from Lorraine to the Belgian coast. They tried to take the offensive, but German trenches were much better built than those of the enemy, which were intended to be temporary before their forces broke through German defences.

"The first thing I saw were two legs sticking out of the ground... There was a skull high up in a tree and helmets with bits of head in them and legs galore."

# Ypres

The main reason for the First Battle of Ypres in November 1914 was the British desire to secure the Channel ports and the army's supply lines. Ypres was the last major obstacle to the German advance on Boulogne-sur-Mer and Calais. The French also wanted to prevent German forces outflanking the Allied front from the north. This was the last major German option after defeats at the Aisne and the Marne.

The battle highlighted problems in command and control for both sides, with each missing opportunities. The Germans overestimated the strength of the Allied defences and called off their last thrust too early. The battle was also the focus of the destruction of the experienced British regular army. Having suffered big losses for its small size, "The Old Contemptibles" disappeared, to be replaced by fresh reserves, which eventually turned into an army of conscripts.

The Allies won, although losses were heavy on both sides. On 22 April 1915, at the Second Battle of Ypres, the Germans (violating the Hague Convention) used chlorine gas for the first time on the Western Front. Several types of gas were soon used by both sides, and though it never proved a winning weapon, poison gas became one of the most-feared and best-remembered horrors of the war.

# Edith Cavell

In November 1914, after the German occupation of Brussels, nurse Edith Cavell began sheltering British soldiers and smuggling them out of occupied Belgium to neutral Holland. Wounded and derelict British and French soldiers and Belgians and French of military age were hidden from the Germans and provided with false papers by Prince Reginald de Croy at his chateau near Mons. From there they were conducted by guides to the houses of Cavell, Louis Séverin and others in Brussels, and given money to reach the Dutch frontier with guides supplied through Phillipe Baucq. This put Cavell in violation of German military law. German authorities became increasingly suspicious of her actions, which were backed up by her outspokenness.

She was arrested on 3 August 1915 and charged with harbouring Allied soldiers. She had been betrayed by Gaston Quien, who was later convicted of collaboration by a French court. (His life sentence was commuted to 20 years in jail. He was released in 1937, still protesting his innocence.) Cavell was held in prison for 10 weeks, the last two in solitary confinement. She made three statements to the German police admitting that she had been instrumental in moving about 60 British and 15 French soldiers and about 100 French and Belgians of military age to the frontier and had sheltered most of them in her house.

She signed a statement the day before her trial and reaffirmed her crime in the presence of other prisoners and lawyers in court at the start of the trial. Cavell gave the German prosecution a much stronger case against her when she declared that the soldiers she had helped escape thanked her in writing when they arrived safely in Britain. This admission proved hard to ignore because it not only confirmed that Cavell had helped the soldiers to navigate the Dutch frontier, but also established that she helped them escape to a country at war with Germany.

The British government said they could do nothing to help her. Cavell was executed.

Cavell was not arrested for espionage, as many were led to believe, but for treason. She had in fact been recruited by the British Secret Intelligence Service, but stopped spying to help Allied soldiers escape.

The night before her execution, she told the Reverend Stirling Gahan, the Anglican chaplain who had been allowed to see her and to give her Holy Communion, "Patriotism is not enough, I must have no hatred or bitterness towards anyone." These words are inscribed on her statue in St Martin's Place, near Trafalgar Square in London.

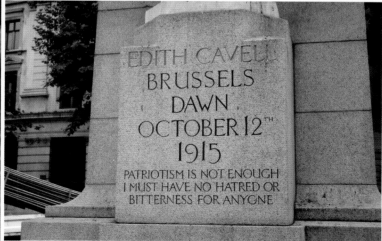

EDITH CAVELL
BRUSSELS
DAWN
OCTOBER 12TH
1915
PATRIOTISM IS NOT ENOUGH
I MUST HAVE NO HATRED OR
BITTERNESS FOR ANYONE

# In the trenches

"The appearance of the trench is atrocious...
In places pools of blood. On the protective wall, in the
communication trench, stiff corpses covered
with tent canvas... An unbearable stench poisons the
air... I have not slept for 72 hours. It is raining."

Charles Delvert, French infantry captain

*Edited from work by English military historian Chris Baker.*

YOUR PAL
IN THE
TRENCHES
IS WAITING TO
SHAKE HANDS
WITH YOU.

## What were the trenches?

Although most of us think primarily of the Great War in terms of life and death in the trenches, only a relatively small proportion of the army actually served there. The trenches were the front lines, the most dangerous places. But behind them was a mass of supply lines, training establishments, stores, workshops, headquarters and all the other elements of the 1914-1918 system of war, in which most troops were employed. The trenches were the domain of the infantry, with the supporting arms of the mortars and machineguns, the engineers and the forward positions of the artillery observers.

## Why were the trenches there?

The idea of digging into the ground to give some protection from powerful enemy artillery and small arms fire was not new. It had been widely practised in the US Civil War, the Russian-Japanese war and other recent wars. Trench warfare can be said to have begun in September 1914 and ended when the Allies made a breakthrough attack in August 1918. Before and after those dates were wars of movement: in between it was a war of entrenchment. The massive armies of 1914 initially fought a war of movement, and any trenches dug were only for temporary cover. But from the Battle of the Aisne onwards, both sides dug in to take cover and hold their ground. The movements to outflank the enemy trenches came to an end by November 1914. By then there was a continuous line of trenches covering 650km from Switzerland to the North Sea. There was no way round.

## What were the trenches like?

The type and nature of the trench positions varied, depending on local conditions. For example, at the River Somme on the Western Front the ground is chalky and is easily dug. The trench sides would crumble after rain, so would be built up ("revetted") with wood, sandbags or any other suitable material. At Ypres, the ground is naturally boggy and the water table high, so trenches were not really dug, but more built up using sandbags and wood ("breastworks"). In parts of Italy, trenches were dug in rock; in Palestine in sand. In France the trenches ran through towns and villages, through industrial works, coalmines, brickyards, across railway tracks, through farms, fields and woods, across rivers, canals and streams. Each feature presented its own challenges for the men who had to dig in and defend. In the major offensives of 1915, 1916 and 1917 many positions were held for only a few days before the next advance moved them on into what had been no man's land or the enemy position. These trenches were scratch affairs, created as the advancing troops dug in, and were sometimes little more than 45cm deep.

A CALL FROM THE TRENCHES

(Extract from a letter from the Trenches.)

"I SAW a recruiting advertisement in a paper the other day. I wonder if the men are responding properly—they would if they could see what the Germans have done in Belgium. And, after all, it's not so bad out here—cold sometimes, and the waiting gets on our nerves a bit, but we are happy and as fit as fiddles. I wonder if ————— has joined, he certainly ought to."

DOES "—————" REFER TO YOU?
IF SO
JOIN
AN IRISH REGIMENT
TO-DAY

The enemy had a similar system. The distance between the two lines varied from as little as 30m to several hundred. The space between the opposing lines was called no man's land. It was difficult to consolidate a captured enemy trench – in effect it had to be turned round because you now needed to have a protected front at what had been the unprotected rear when the enemy held it.

As defensive and offensive tactics developed, trench positions became formidable fortresses with barbed wire belts tens of metres deep in front of them, with concrete shelters and emplacements, often below ground level. Machineguns would be permanently trained on gaps deliberately left in the wire, and the artillery would also have the positions registered for firing at short notice.

## Living conditions.

Where possible, the floor of the trench was made with wooden duckboards. Latrines had to be dug somewhere close. This was generally as deep a hole in the ground as possible, over which was mounted a plank to sit on. Men would, with permission, leave their post to use the latrine. This rough form of sanitation was often a target for enemy snipers and shellfire and was a considerable smell and health hazard for the men in the trenches.

Trench conditions varied widely between different theatres, different sectors within a theatre, and with the time of year and weather. Trench life was, however, always one of considerable squalor, with so many men living in a very constrained space. Scraps of discarded food, empty tins and other waste, the nearby presence of the latrine, the general dirt of living half underground and being unable to wash or change for days or weeks at a time created conditions of severe health risk (and that is not counting the military risks). Vermin, including rats and lice, were numerous; disease was spread both by them and by the maggots and flies that thrived on the nearby remains of decomposing human and animal corpses. Troops in the trenches were also subjected to the weather: the winter of 1916-1917 in France and Flanders was the coldest in memory; the trenches flooded, sometimes to waist height, whenever it rained. Men suffered from exposure, frostbite, trench foot (a wasting disease of the flesh caused by the foot being wet and cold, constrained into boots and puttees, for days on end), and many diseases brought on or made worse by living in such a way.

## How long would a man have to be in a trench?

A general pattern for trench routine was four days in the front line, then four days in close reserve and finally four at rest, although this varied with the conditions, the weather and the availability of enough reserve troops to be able to rotate them this way. In close reserve, men had to be ready to reinforce the line at short notice. They may have been in a trench system just behind the front system or in the dubious shelter of a ruined

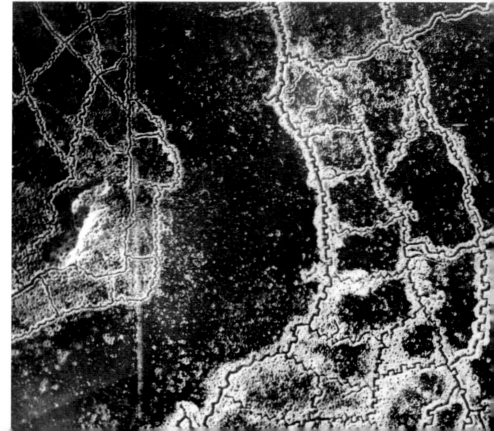

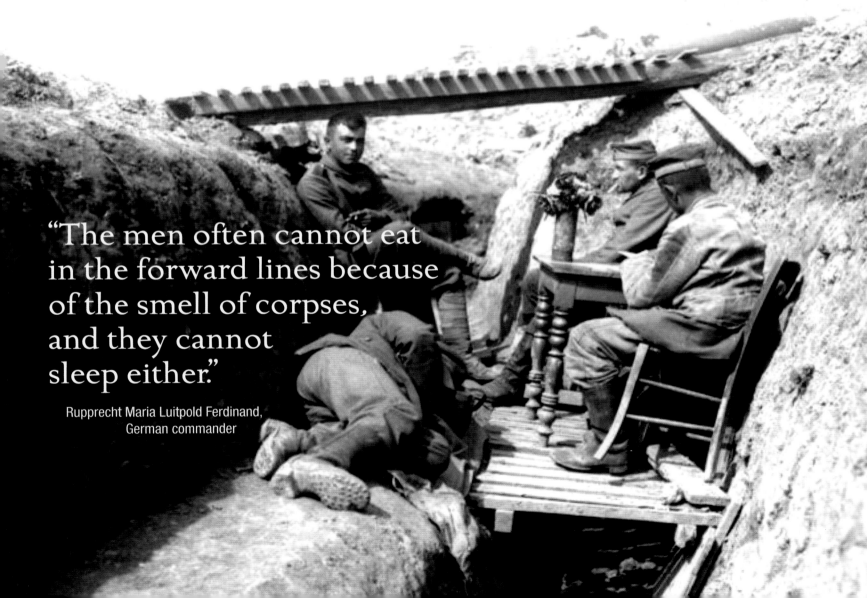

"The men often cannot eat in the forward lines because of the smell of corpses, and they cannot sleep either."

Rupprecht Maria Luitpold Ferdinand, German commander

village or wood. The relief of a unit after its time in the front by a fresh one was always an anxious time, as the noise and obvious activity increased the risk of attracting enemy attention in the form of shelling, machinegun fire or even a raid at the very time when the manning of the position was changing. Once the incoming unit had relieved the outgoing one, precautionary actions would be taken. At least one man in four (at night, and perhaps one in 10 by day) were posted as sentries on look-out duty, often in saps dug a little way ahead of the main fire trench. They would listen for sounds that might indicate enemy activity, and try to observe such activity across no man's land. The other men would be posted into the fire trench or support trench in sections. Unless they were a specialist such as a signaller or machinegunner, men would inevitably be assigned to carrying, repair or digging parties, or sent under cover of dark to put out or repair barbed wire defences.

Other than when a major action was under way, trench life was usually tedious and hard physical work. Officers had to try to ensure that there was a balance between the need for work against the enemy, on building and repairing trench defences, and for rest and sleep. This could only be done by a definite system of rotas and a work timetable. Obviously, in times of battle or extended alerts, such a routine would be broken, but such times were a small proportion of the time in the trenches. The main enemies were the weather and boredom. The loss of concentration – leaving oneself exposed to sniper fire, for example – could prove deadly. At dawn and dusk, the whole British line was ordered to Stand to!, which meant a period of manning the trench in preparation for an enemy attack.

All the men posted to the fire trench and most of those in the support trench had to wear their equipment at all times. Men in the front line had to keep their bayonets fixed during darkness or mist, or whenever there was an alert of enemy activity. A man could not leave his post without permission from his immediate commander, and an officer had to approve him leaving the trench. One officer per company was on trench duty at all times, and his NCOs had to report to him hourly. He was under orders to move continually up and down his assigned trenches, checking that the equipment was in good state, that the sentries were alert and that the men were as comfortable as the conditions allowed. The NCOs had to inspect the men's rifles twice daily and otherwise ensure that fighting equipment and ammunition was present and in good order. From mid-1915, every trench had some form of warning of gas attack. Often this was an empty shell casing, held up by wire or

The War Illustrated, 13th March, 1915.

Simple Life in British Trench "Hotels"

After dinner in the trenches, nicknamed "Pall Mall" and "Piccadilly." A peaceful pipe round the glowing brazier during a lull in the firing.

Our soldiers call their dug-outs the "Ritz Restaurant," or the "Carlton Hotel." A sand-bag "lounge!"

Practically the only kind of bath that is known to those on duty in the muddy trenches.

The "Café de l'Europe!" Mud-caked, cold, and wet—but ever-cheerful, British soldier eating his dinner of bully-beef outside a "funk-hole."

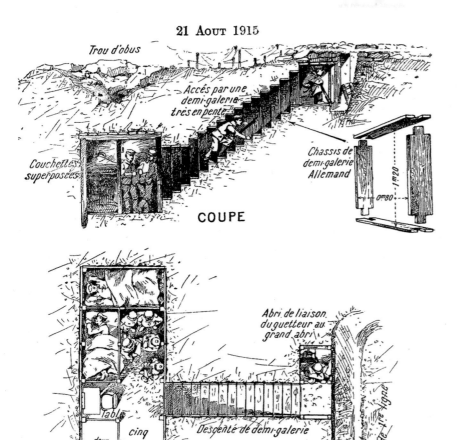

21 Août 1915

Trou d'obus

Accès par une demi-galerie très en pente

Couchettes superposées

COUPE

Chassis de demi-galerie Allemand

0m80 · 1m20

Abri de liaison du guetteur au grand abri

Table

deux couchettes superposées

cinq hommes debout

Descente de demi-galerie

deux couchettes superposées

Niche du guetteur avec banc

Tranchée de 1re ligne

PLAN

e d'abri allemand en première ligne, avec accès par une demi-galerie en escalier.

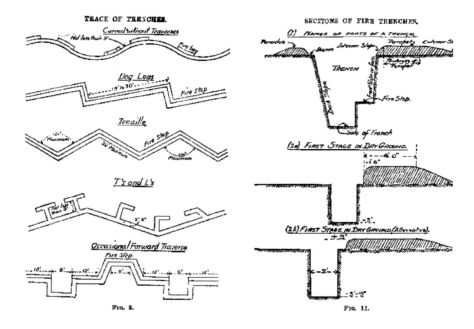

string, that would be hit like a gong with a piece of wood or similar. If the gas gong was heard, all officers and men would know that they had to put on their gas masks.

Every day, the battalion holding the line would request from the nearby brigade workshop a list of stores it needed. Some special items such as wire "knife rests" (a wooden support for a barbed wire entanglement), signboards, boxes and floor gratings would be made up at brigade and brought to the trenches ready to use. Sandbags, wood, cement, barbed wire, telephone cable, and other supplies would also be sent up as needed. Men would be sent back to brigade as a carrying party to fetch it.

Rations and other supplies were invariably brought up at night, under cover of darkness. This was of course known to the enemy, who would shell and snipe at the known roads and tracks leading up to the front. The units holding the front would try to position their mobile field cookers so that the men could be provided with a hot meal, but this was not always possible. The men in the trenches would also cook – especially breakfast – using braziers in the trenches and dugouts. It was important that smoke from fires was masked so as not to give away a position.

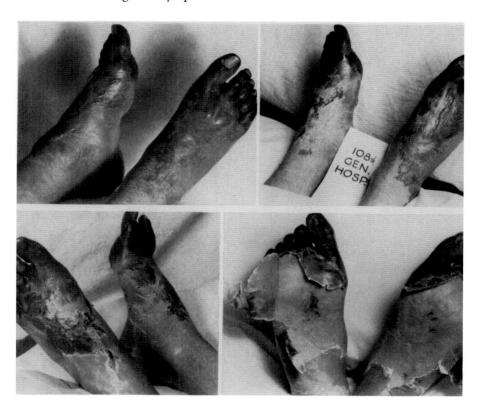

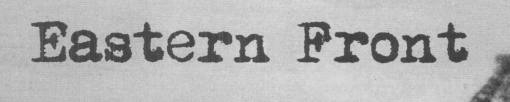

"I didn't get much peace, but I heard in
Norway that Russia might well
become a huge market for tractors soon."

Henry Ford, after a failed 'peace mission' to Europe, 1915

While the Western Front had reached stalemate, the war continued in eastern Europe. Russian plans called for simultaneous invasions of Austrian Galicia and German East Prussia. Although Russia's advance into Galicia was largely successful, it was driven back from East Prussia by Hindenburg and Ludendorff in August and September 1914. Russia's less developed industrial base and ineffective military leadership were instrumental in the events that unfolded. By the spring of 1915, the Russians had retreated from Galicia and, in May, the Central Powers broke through on Poland's southern frontiers. On 5 August they captured Warsaw and forced the Russians to withdraw from Poland.

# The Battle of Verdun

For almost all of 1916 – from 21 February to 18 December – on hills north of Verdun-sur-Meuse in north-eastern France, German and French forces tried to annihilate each other.

The German strategy was to provoke the French into counter-attacks and counter-offensives to drive them off the heights. These would have been easy to repel with fire from the medium, heavy and super-heavy guns, supplied with large amounts of ammunition on excellent pre-war railways, which ran within 24km of the front line.

Bad weather held up the start of the German offensive until 21 February. French construction of defensive lines and the arrival of reinforcements before the opening attack were able to delay the German advance. By 6 March, 20 French divisions were in the area and deep defence had been established. The commander of the French Second Army, General Philippe Pétain, ordered that no withdrawals be made and that counter-attacks be conducted, despite exposing French infantry to fire. By 29 March French artillery on the west bank had begun a constant bombardment of German positions on the east bank.

In March the German offensive was extended to the west bank so they could see the ground from which French artillery had been firing. The Germans made substantial advances, but French reinforcements contained them. In early May the Germans changed tactics and made local attacks and counter-attacks, which gave the French an opportunity to attack Fort Douaumont, which was partially occupied, until a German counter-attack reoccupied the fort and took prisoners. The Germans changed tactics again, alternating between both banks of the Meuse, and in June captured Fort Vaux. They continued beyond Fort Vaux, drove into the French defences, took Fleury and brought the front line within 4km of the Verdun citadel.

The German offensive was reduced to provide reinforcements for the Somme, where the Anglo-French relief offensive began on 1 July. During the fighting Fleury changed hands 16 times from 23 June–17 August. A final German attempt to capture Fort Souville in early July reached the fort, but was repulsed by counter-attacks. The German offensive was reduced further, although an attempt was made to deceive the French into expecting more attacks, to keep them away from the Somme front. In August and December French counter-offensives recaptured much of the ground lost on the east bank and recovered Douaumont and Vaux. A recent estimate found 976,000 casualties during the Battle of Verdun, an average of 97,000 a month.

"Shrieks of agony and groans all around me...
All about me are bits of men and ghastly
mixtures of cloth and blood."

Anthony R. Hossack, British soldier

# The Somme

More than a million men were killed or wounded during the Battle of the Somme. It was one of humankind's bloodiest battles.

The Allies agreed on offensives in 1916 by the French, Russian, British and Italian armies, with a Somme offensive as the Franco-British contribution. The main part of the offensive was to be made by the French Army, supported on the north by the Fourth Army of the British Expeditionary Force.

But when the German Army began the Battle of Verdun, French divisions intended for the Somme were diverted and the supporting attack by the British at the Somme became the main effort.

The first day saw a serious defeat for the German Second Army, which was forced out of its first line of defence by the French Sixth Army, from Foucaucourt-en-Santerre south of the Somme to Maricourt on the north bank and by the British Fourth Army from Maricourt to near the Albert–Bapaume road.

The first day of July 1916 was also the worst day in the history of the British Army, which had 60,000 casualties, mainly between the Albert–Bapaume road and Gommecourt, where the attack failed disastrously. The British Army on the Somme was a mixture of the remnants of the pre-war regular army and the Territorial Force and the men of the Kitchener Army, who were recruited from the same towns and occupations. Their losses had a profound impact in Britain.

"What a slaughter. Hell cannot be this dreadful."

Alfred Joubaire, French lieutenant

The Somme battle is notable for the use of air power and the tank. By the end, the British and French had penetrated 10km into occupied territory, taking more ground than in any offensive since the Marne in 1914. The Anglo-French armies had failed to capture Péronne and were still 5km from Bapaume, where the German armies dug in for winter. British attacks in the Ancre valley resumed in January 1917 and forced the Germans into local withdrawals to reserve lines in February before the scheduled retirement to the Hindenburg Line began in March.

The commander of the BEF, General Sir Douglas Haig, and the commander of the Fourth Army, General Henry Rawlinson, have been criticised ever since for the human cost of the battle and for failing to achieve their territorial objectives. On 1 August 1916 Winston Churchill criticised the British Army's conduct of the offensive to the British Cabinet, claiming that though the battle had forced the Germans to end their offensive at Verdun, attrition was damaging the British armies more than the German.

The entire Somme offensive cost the British Army 420,000 men. The French suffered another estimated 200,000 casualties and the Germans an estimated 500,000. The action at Verdun through 1916, combined with the bloodletting at the Somme, brought the French army to the brink of collapse. Attempts at frontal assault came at a high price for both the British and the French.

The British Battle of Arras was more limited in scope, and more successful, although of little strategic value. A smaller part of the Arras offensive, the capture of Vimy Ridge by the Canadian Corps, became significant to that country: the idea that Canada's national identity was born out of the battle is an opinion widely held in military and general histories of Canada.

The last large-scale offensive of this period was a British attack (with French support) at Passchendaele (July–November 1917). This opened with great promise for the Allies, before bogging down in the October mud. Casualties, though disputed, were about equal, at 200,000–400,000 each.

These years of trench warfare in the West saw no major exchanges of territory and, as a result, are often thought of as static and unchanging. However, British, French and German tactics constantly evolved to meet new battlefield challenges.

"What is our task? To make Britain a fit country for heroes to live in."

David Lloyd George

# Mata Hari

On 13 February 1917, Margaretha Geertruida "M'greet" Zelle MacLeod, an exotic dancer who used the stage name Mata Hari, was arrested in her hotel room on the Champs Elysée in Paris. She was put on trial on 24 July, accused of spying for Germany and causing the deaths of 50,000 soldiers. Although the French and British intelligence suspected her of spying, neither could find evidence. Secret ink was found in her room, which was incriminating, but she said it was part of her make-up. She wrote several letters to the Dutch Consul in Paris, claiming her innocence. "My international connections are due of my work as a dancer, nothing else…. Because I really did not spy, it is terrible that I cannot defend myself." Her defence lawyer, Edouard Clunet, faced huge odds: he could not cross-examine the prosecution's witnesses or directly question his own witnesses. In the circumstances, her conviction was a foregone conclusion. She was executed by firing squad on 15 October 1917, at the age of 41.

German documents unsealed in the 1970s proved that Mata Hari was truly a German agent. In the autumn of 1915 she entered German service, and was taught her duties by a Major Roepell in Cologne. Her reports were to be sent to the War News Post West in Düsseldorf under Roepell and to the agent mission in the German embassy in Madrid.

In December 1916, the French War Ministry let Mata Hari obtain the names of six Belgian agents. Five were suspected of working for the Germans, while the sixth was suspected of being a double agent for Germany and France. Two weeks after Mata Hari had left Paris for a trip to Madrid, the double agent was executed by the Germans, while the five others continued their operations. This development served as proof to the French that Mata Hari had given the names of the six to the Germans.

An eyewitness, British reporter Henry Wales, said she was not bound and refused a blindfold at her execution. Wales said that after the shots rang out "Slowly, inertly, she settled to her knees, her head up always, and without the slightest change of expression on her face. For the fraction of a second it seemed she tottered there, on her knees, gazing directly at those who had taken her life. Then she fell backward, bending at the waist, with her legs doubled up beneath her". A non-commissioned officer then walked up to her body, pulled out his revolver, and shot her in the head to make sure she was dead.

# The sad case of Private Harry Farr

Harry Farr was born in London in 1891. He joined the British Expeditionary Force in 1914 and fought in the trenches. His position was repeatedly shelled, and in May 1915 he collapsed with convulsions. In hospital, his wife Gertrude (who died in 1993 aged 99), who was denied a widow's pension after the war, recalled, "He shook all the time. He couldn't stand the noise of the guns. We got a letter from him, but it was in a stranger's handwriting. He could write perfectly well, but couldn't hold the pen because his hand was shaking."

It is now thought that Farr was suffering from hyperacusis, which occurs when part of the inner ear is damaged by sound, causing it to lose its ability to soften and filter sound, making loud noises physically unbearable. Despite this, Farr was sent back to the front and fought at the Somme. After several months of fighting, he asked to see a medical orderly, but was refused.

After he refused to return to the front line, Farr was court-martialled, during which he had to defend himself. This lasted only 20 minutes, and questions have been raised about its competence. General Sir Douglas Haig signed his death warrant and he was shot at dawn on 18 October 1916. His family always argued that he was suffering from shell shock. He was tried in court for misbehaving before the enemy in such a manner as to show cowardice and found guilty.

Soldiers in the firing squad were tormented by the experience for the rest of their lives. John Laister recalled how he and others were marched into the woods and told they were to be part of a firing squad. He said he was still haunted by the moment that he looked in the direction the rifles were pointed and saw a mere boy with his back to a tree. "There were tears in his eyes and tears in mine."

Gertrude Farr was told her husband had been killed in action, but later when her pension was stopped she was told he had been shot for cowardice and she was not entitled to it. In 1992, Gertrude and her family discovered that that an MP was involved in a campaign for justice for those in similar positions to Farr. When they got the court martial papers they were horrified to discover that Farr had been sent back to the front, when he in fact needed treatment.

Despite a sustained campaign, Prime Minister John Major refused a pardon. In 1993 Gertrude Farr died.

On 15 August 2006, Harry Farr's family announced that he was to be granted a pardon – as one of 306 British Empire soldiers executed for certain offences during the war.

# Southern theatres

"All day long they lie there, being decimated, getting themselves killed next to the bodies of those killed earlier."

French officer

# The Balkans

Serbia was conquered in little more than a month, as the Central Powers, including Bulgaria, sent in 600,000 troops. The Serbian army, fighting on two fronts and facing certain defeat, retreated into northern Albania. The Serbs suffered defeat in the Battle of Kosovo. Montenegro covered the Serbian retreat towards the Adriatic coast in the Battle of Mojkovac in 6–7 January 1916, but ultimately the Austrians conquered Montenegro, too. The surviving Serbian soldiers were evacuated by ship to Greece. After conquest, Serbia was divided between Austro-Hungary and Bulgaria.

In late 1915, a Franco-British force landed at Salonika in Greece to offer help and to press the government to declare war against the Central Powers. However, the pro-German King Constantine I dismissed his pro-Allied government. The friction between Constantine and the Allies continued to grow, and Greece was divided between regions loyal to the king and the new pro-Allies provisional government in Salonika. After an armed confrontation in Athens, Constantine resigned and his second son, Alexander took his place; Greece then officially joined the war on the side of the Allies.

Serbian and French troops finally broke through the Macedonian front in September 1918 after most of the German and Austro-Hungarian troops had withdrawn. Bulgaria caved in on 29 September. The Germans responded by sending troops to hold the line, but the force was far too weak to re-establish a front.

The disappearance of the Macedonian Front meant that the road to Budapest and Vienna was now open to Allied forces. Hindenburg and Ludendorff concluded that the strategic and operational balance had shifted against the Central Powers and, a day after the Bulgarian collapse, insisted on an immediate peace settlement.

# Ottoman Empire

The Ottoman Empire joined the Central Powers in the war; the secret Ottoman–German Alliance having been signed in August 1914. It threatened Russia's Caucasian territories and Britain's communications with India via the Suez Canal. The British and French opened overseas fronts with the Gallipoli (1915) and Mesopotamian campaigns.

In Gallipoli, the Ottoman Empire successfully repelled the British, French and Australian and New Zealand Army Corps (Anzacs). In Mesopotamia, by contrast, after the disastrous Siege of Kut (1915–16), British Imperial forces reorganised and captured Baghdad in March 1917.

Farther west, the Suez Canal was successfully defended from Ottoman attacks in 1915 and 1916. In August, a joint German and Ottoman force was defeated at the Battle of Romani by the Anzac Mounted and the 52nd (Lowland) Infantry Divisions. After this victory, a British Empire Egyptian Expeditionary Force advanced across the Sinai Peninsula, pushing Ottoman forces back in the Battle of Magdhaba in December and the Battle of Rafa on the border between the Egyptian Sinai and Ottoman Palestine in January 1917.

Russian armies generally had the best of it in the Caucasus. Enver Pasha, supreme commander of the Ottoman armed forces, dreamed of reconquering central Asia and areas that had been lost to Russia. He was, however, a poor commander. He launched an offensive against the Russians in the Caucasus in December 1914 with 100,000 troops, but insisting on a frontal attack against mountainous Russian positions in winter he lost 86 per cent of his force.

General Nikolai Yudenich, Russian commander from 1915 to 1916, drove the Turks out of most of the southern Caucasus with a string of victories. In 1917, Russian Grand Duke Nicholas assumed command of the Caucasus front. He planned a railway from Russian Georgia to the conquered territories so fresh supplies could be brought up for a new offensive in 1917. However, in March 1917 (February in the pre-revolutionary Russian calendar), the tsar abdicated in the course of the February Revolution and the Russian Caucasus Army began to fall apart.

In March and April 1917, at the Battles of Gaza, German and Ottoman forces stopped the advance of the Egyptian Expeditionary Force, which had begun in August 1916 at Romani. At the end of October, the Sinai and Palestine Campaign resumed when General Edmund Allenby's XXth Corps, XXI Corps and Desert Mounted Corps won the Battle of Beersheba. Two Ottoman armies were defeated a few weeks later at the Battle of Mughar Ridge and, early in December, Jerusalem was captured after another Ottoman defeat at the Battle of Jerusalem (1917).

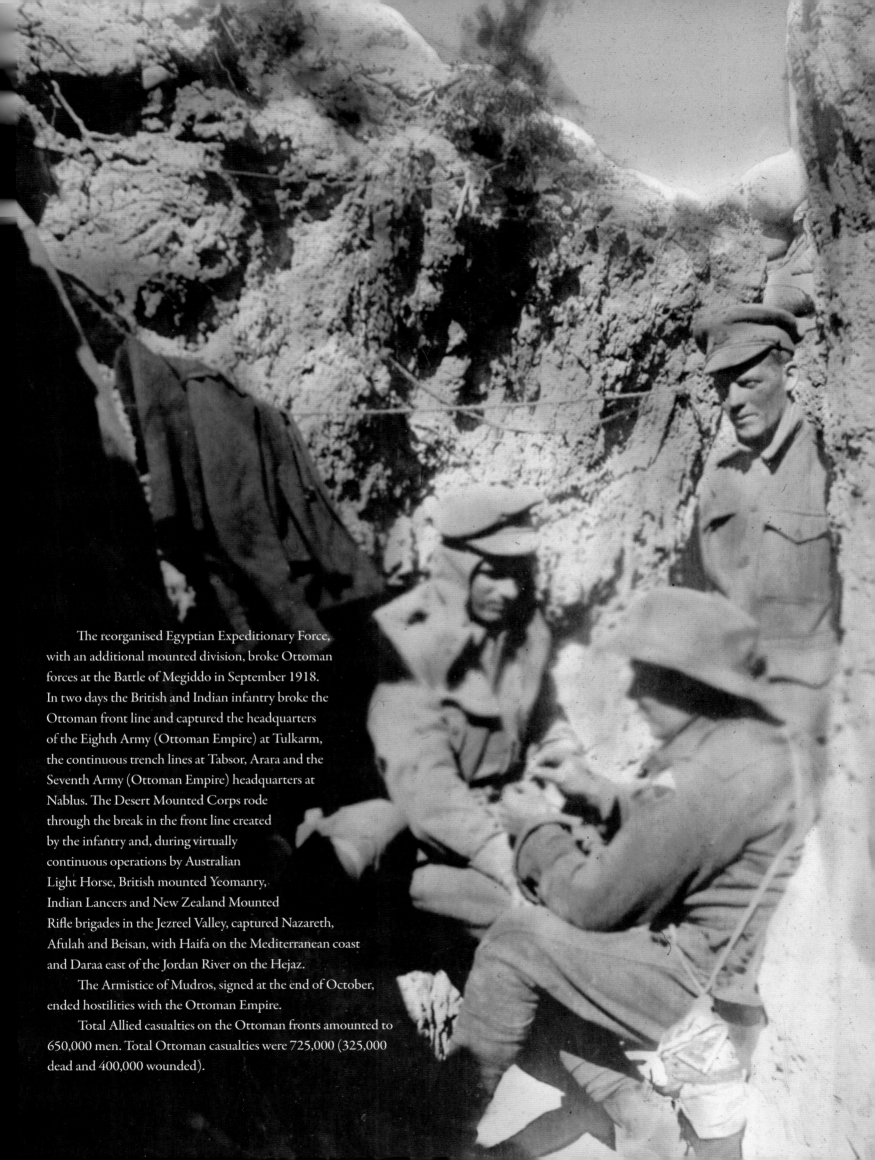

The reorganised Egyptian Expeditionary Force, with an additional mounted division, broke Ottoman forces at the Battle of Megiddo in September 1918. In two days the British and Indian infantry broke the Ottoman front line and captured the headquarters of the Eighth Army (Ottoman Empire) at Tulkarm, the continuous trench lines at Tabsor, Arara and the Seventh Army (Ottoman Empire) headquarters at Nablus. The Desert Mounted Corps rode through the break in the front line created by the infantry and, during virtually continuous operations by Australian Light Horse, British mounted Yeomanry, Indian Lancers and New Zealand Mounted Rifle brigades in the Jezreel Valley, captured Nazareth, Afulah and Beisan, with Haifa on the Mediterranean coast and Daraa east of the Jordan River on the Hejaz.

The Armistice of Mudros, signed at the end of October, ended hostilities with the Ottoman Empire.

Total Allied casualties on the Ottoman fronts amounted to 650,000 men. Total Ottoman casualties were 725,000 (325,000 dead and 400,000 wounded).

# Gallipoli

Needing a sea route to Russia, the British and French launched a naval campaign to force a passage through the Dardanelles. An amphibious landing was also made on the Gallipoli peninsula to capture the Ottoman capital of Constantinople (Istanbul). After eight months the land campaign failed, with many casualties on both sides, and the invasion force was withdrawn to Egypt.

The campaign was one of the greatest Ottoman victories of the war and is considered a major failure by the Allies. In Turkey, it is perceived as a defining moment in the nation's history – a final surge in the defence of the motherland as the Ottoman Empire crumbled.

The struggle formed the basis for the Turkish War of Independence and the founding of the Republic of Turkey eight years later under Mustafa Kemal Atatürk, a commander at Gallipoli. The campaign is also considered to mark the birth of national consciousness in Australia and New Zealand and the date of the landing, 25 April, is known as Anzac Day. It remains the most significant commemoration of military casualties and veterans there, surpassing Remembrance Day (Armistice Day).

# Simpson and his donkey

Stretcher-bearer John Simpson Kirkpatrick landed on the shores of the Gallipoli Peninsula on 25 April 1915 as part of the Anzac forces. In the early hours of the next day, as he was bearing a wounded comrade on his shoulders, he saw a donkey and quickly began making use of it to bear his fellow soldiers. He would sing and whistle, seeming to ignore the deadly bullets flying through the air, while he tended to wounded mens. The donkey came to be named Duffy.

Colonel (later General) John Monash wrote: "Private Simpson and his little beast earned the admiration of everyone at the upper end of the valley. They worked all day and night throughout the whole period since the landing, and the help rendered to the wounded was invaluable. Simpson knew no fear and moved unconcernedly amid shrapnel and rifle fire, steadily carrying out his self-imposed task day by day, and he frequently earned the applause of the personnel for his many fearless rescues of wounded men from areas subject to rifle and shrapnel fire."

On 19 May 1915, Simpson was struck by machinegun fire and died.

THE MAP SHOWS THE ENTIRE ZONE OF ACTIVE OPERATIONS ON THE WESTERN AND ITALIAN FRONTS. THOUGH SPOKEN OF AS SEPARATE, THEY FORM IN REALITY ONE FRONT, AS A DISASTER TO THE ITALIAN LINE ENABLING THE GERMANS TO REACH CENTRAL ITALY WOULD HAVE IMMEDIATELY REACTED CALAMITOUSLY ON THE ALLIES FIGHTING IN FRANCE AND BELGIUM.

MEN WHO MATTER IN ITALY
THE PERSONAL SIDE OF THE WAR

# Italy

Despite its Triple Alliance with the German and Austro-Hungarian empires, Italy had designs on Austrian territory. Rome had a secret 1902 pact with France, effectively nullifying the alliance. At the start of the war, Italy refused to commit troops, arguing that the alliance was defensive and that Austria-Hungary was an aggressor.

The Austro-Hungarian government began negotiations to secure Italian neutrality, offering the French colony of Tunisia in return. The Allies made a counter-offer in which Italy would receive the Southern Tyrol, the Julian March and territory on the Dalmatian coast after the defeat of Austria-Hungary, which was formalised by the Treaty of London. Further encouraged by the Allied invasion of Turkey in April 1915, Italy joined the Triple Entente and declared war on Austria-Hungary on 23 May. Fifteen months later, Italy declared war on Germany.

Italy's entry was engineered in secret by three men – the Prime Minister, Antonio Salandra, the Foreign Minister, Sidney Sonnino, and King Victor Emmanuel III.

On 16 February 1915, despite negotiations with Austria, a courier was sent secretly to London with the suggestion that Italy was open to a good offer. After Russian victories in the Carpathians, Salandra began to think victory for the Entente was in sight, and was so anxious not to arrive too late for a share in the profits that he instructed his envoy in London to drop some demands and reach agreement quickly. The Treaty of London was concluded on 26 April, binding Italy to fight within a month.

Field Marshal Luigi Cadorna, a proponent of the frontal assault, dreamt of breaking into the Slovenian plateau, taking Ljubljana and threatening Vienna. The plan did not take into account the rugged alps or the technological changes that had created trench warfare, giving rise to a series of bloody stalemates.

The Austro-Hungarians took advantage of the mountains, which favoured the defender. After a strategic retreat, the front remained largely unchanged, while the Austrians engaged the Italians in hand-to-hand combat throughout the summer.

The Central Powers launched a crushing offensive on 26 October 1917, spearheaded by the Germans. The Italian Army was routed at Caporetto and retreated more than 100km to reorganise. In 1918, the Austro-Hungarians failed to break through in a series of battles on the Piave River, and were finally beaten in the Battle of Vittorio Veneto in October. From 5–6 November 1918, Italian forces were reported to have reached the Dalmatian coast. By the end of hostilities in November 1918, the Italian military had seized the entire portion of Dalmatia that had been guaranteed to Italy by the London Pact. In 1918, Admiral Enrico Millo declared himself Italy's Governor of Dalmatia.

# Romania

Romania had been allied with the Central Powers since 1882, but when the war began it declared neutrality, arguing that because Austria-Hungary had itself declared war on Serbia, Romania was under no obligation to join in. When the Entente Powers promised it large parts of eastern Hungary, which had a large Romanian population, in exchange for Romania's declaring war on the Central Powers, the Romanian government renounced its neutrality and, on 27 August 1916, attacked Austria-Hungary, with limited Russian support. The Romanian offensive was initially successful, pushing back the Austro-Hungarian troops in Transylvania, but a counterattack by the Central Powers drove back the Russo-Romanians. After the Battle of Bucharest, the Central Powers occupied the city on 6 December 1916. Russian withdrawal from the war in late 1917 as a result of the October Revolution meant Romania had to sign an armistice with the Central Powers on 9 December 1917.

The treaty was renounced in October 1918 by the Romanian government, and Romania nominally re-entered the war on 10 November 1918. The next day, the Treaty of Bucharest was nullified by the terms of the Armistice. Total Romanian deaths from 1914 to 1918, military and civilian, within contemporary borders, were estimated at 748,000.

# Africa

On 7 August 1914, French and British troops invaded the German protectorate of Togoland. On 10 August, German forces in South-West Africa attacked South Africa. Sporadic fierce fighting continued for the rest of the war. The German colonial forces in German East Africa, led by Colonel Paul von Lettow-Vorbeck, fought a guerrilla campaign and did not surrender until two weeks after the armistice took effect in Europe.

# Russian Revolution

In March 1917, demonstrations in Petrograd culminated in the abdication of Tsar Nicholas II and the appointment of a provisional government, which shared power with the Soviet socialists. This led to confusion both at the front and at home. The army became increasingly ineffective.

Discontent and the weaknesses of the provisional government increased the popularity of the Bolshevik Party, led by Vladimir Lenin, which demanded an immediate end to the war. The successful armed uprising by the Bolsheviks in November was followed in December by an armistice and negotiations with Germany. At first, the Bolsheviks refused the German terms, but when German troops began marching across Ukraine unopposed, the new government acceded to the Treaty of Brest-Litovsk on 3 March 1918. The treaty ceded vast territories, including Finland, the Baltic provinces, parts of Poland and Ukraine, to the Central Powers. Despite this enormous apparent German success, the manpower required for occupation of the territory may have contributed to the failure of the Spring Offensive and secured relatively little food or other materiel.

# Asia and the Pacific

New Zealand occupied German Samoa (now Samoa) on 30 August 1914. On 11 September, the Australian Naval and Military Expeditionary Force landed on what is now New Britain, which formed part of German New Guinea. On 28 October, the German cruiser *Emden* sank the Russian cruiser *Zhemchug* in the Battle of Penang. Japan seized Germany's Micronesian colonies and the German coaling port of Qingdao in the Chinese Shandong peninsula. As Vienna refused to withdraw the Austro-Hungarian cruiser *Kaiserin Elisabeth* from Tsingtao, Japan declared war not only on Germany, but also on Austria-Hungary. The ship took part in the defence of Tsingtao, where it was sunk in November 1914. Within a few months, the Allied forces had seized all German territories in the Pacific. Only isolated commerce raiders and a few holdouts in New Guinea remained.

# Indian support

The outbreak of the war saw an outpouring of Indian loyalty and goodwill towards Britain. Leaders from the Indian National Congress and other groups were eager to support the British, believing that would further their case for Indian Home Rule. About 1.3 million Indian soldiers and labourers served in Europe, Africa, and the Middle East, while both the central government and the princely states sent food, money and ammunition. In all, 140,000 men served on the Western Front and nearly 700,000 in the Middle East. Casualties totalled 47,746 killed and 65,126 wounded. The suffering, as well as the failure of the British government to grant self-government to India after the war, bred disillusionment and fuelled the campaign for independence led by Mohandas Gandhi and others.

# Ground warfare

World War I began as a clash of 20th-century technology and 19th-century tactics, with inevitable large casualties. By the end of 1917, however, the major armies, numbering millions of men, had modernised and were using the telephone, wireless, armoured cars, tanks and aircraft. Infantry formations were reorganised so 100-man companies were no longer the main unit. Instead, squads of 10 or so men, under the command of a junior NCO, were favoured.

Artillery also underwent a revolution. In 1914, cannons were in the front line and fired straight at their targets. By 1917, indirect fire with cannon (as well as mortars and machineguns) was commonplace, with new techniques for spotting and ranging, including aircraft and the often overlooked field telephone. Counter-battery missions became common and sound detection was used to find enemy batteries.

Germany was far ahead of the Allies in using heavy indirect fire. The German Army used 150mm and 210mm howitzers in 1914, when typical French and British guns were only 75mm and 105mm. The British had a 152mm howitzer, but it was so heavy it had to be hauled to the field in pieces and assembled.

Artillery was responsible for most casualties and used vast quantities of explosives. The many head wounds caused by exploding shells and fragmentation forced the combatant nations to develop the modern steel helmet, led by the French, who introduced the Adrian helmet in 1915. It was quickly followed by the Brodie helmet, worn by British Imperial and US troops, and in 1916 by the distinctive German *Stahlhelm*, a design, with improvements, still in use today.

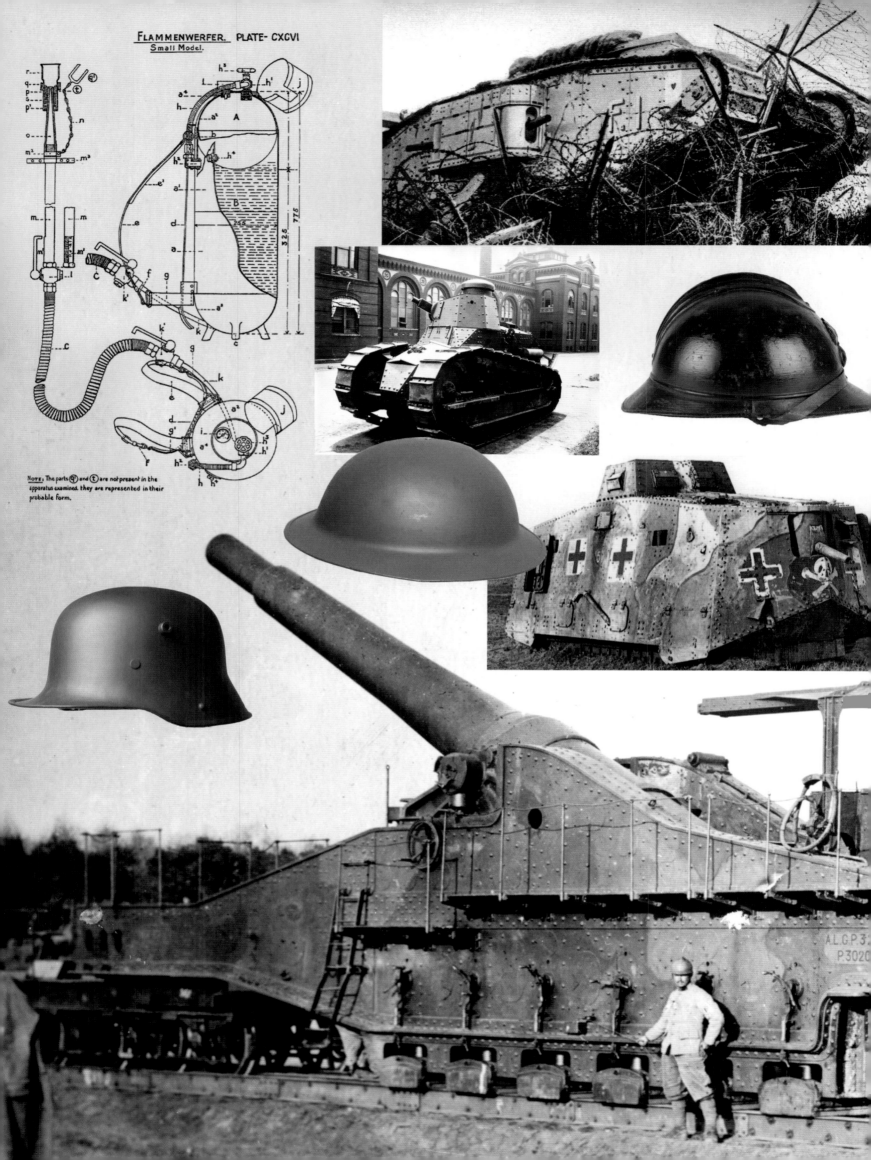

FLAMMENWERFER. PLATE- CXCVI
Small Model.

Note. The parts q and t are not present in the apparatus examined. they are represented in their probable form.

AL.G.P.3
P3020

The use of chemicals was a distinguishing feature of the conflict. Gases used included chlorine, mustard gas and phosgene. Gas caused few casualties, as countermeasures were quickly created, such as gas masks.

The most powerful land weapons were railway guns weighing hundreds of tonnes each. These were nicknamed Big Berthas, even though the gun they were named after was not a railway gun. Germany developed the Paris Gun, able to bombard Paris from over 100km, though shells were relatively light at 94kg. While the Allies also had railway guns, German models severely out-ranged and out-classed them.

Trenches, machineguns, air reconnaissance, barbed wire, and modern artillery with fragmentation shells helped bring the battle lines of the war to a stalemate. The British and the French sought a solution with the creation of the tank and mechanised warfare. The first British tanks were used during the Battle of the Somme on 15 September 1916. Mechanical reliability was an issue, but the experiment proved its worth. Within a year, the British were using hundreds of tanks. They showed their potential during the Battle of Cambrai in November 1917 by breaking the Hindenburg Line, while combined arms teams captured 8000 enemy soldiers and 100 guns.

The French introduced the first tanks with a rotating turret, the Renault FT, which became a decisive tool of the victory. The conflict also saw the introduction of light automatic weapons and sub-machineguns, such as the Lewis Gun, the Browning automatic rifle, and the Bergmann MP18.

Another new weapon, the flamethrower, was first used by the German army and later adopted by others. Although not of high tactical value, the flamethrower was a powerful, demoralising weapon that caused terror on the battlefield. It was a dangerous weapon to wield, as its weight made operators vulnerable.

# The war at sea

The German Navy used U-boats to deprive the British Isles of vital supplies. The deaths of British merchant sailors and the apparent invulnerability of U-boats led to the development of depth charges (1916), hydrophones (passive sonar, 1917), blimps, hunter-killer submarines (HMS *R-1*, 1917), forward-throwing anti-submarine weapons and dipping hydrophones (the latter two both abandoned in 1918). To extend their operations, the Germans proposed supply submarines (1916). Most of these were forgotten in the interwar period until World War ll revived the need.

At the start of the war, the German Empire had cruisers scattered across the globe, some of which were later used to attack Allied merchant ships. The Royal Navy hunted them down, though not without some embarrassment from its inability to protect Allied shipping. For example, the German light cruiser *Emden*, part of the East-Asia squadron stationed at Qingdao, seized or destroyed 15 merchantmen and sank a Russian cruiser and a French destroyer. However, most of the German East-Asia squadron – the cruisers *Scharnhorst* and *Gneisenau*, light cruisers *Nurnberg* and *Leipzig* and two transport ships – did not have orders to raid

shipping and was instead on the way to Germany when it met British warships. The German flotilla and *Dresden* sank two armoured cruisers at the Battle of Coronel, but were almost destroyed at the Battle of the Falkland Islands in December 1914, with only *Dresden* and a few auxiliaries escaping, but at the Battle of Mas a Tierra these too were destroyed or interned.

Soon after the start of the war Britain began a naval blockade of Germany. This proved effective, cutting off vital military and civilian supplies. Britain mined international waters to prevent ships entering entire sections of ocean, causing danger to even neutral ships.

The 1916 Battle of Jutland developed into the largest naval battle and the only full-scale clash of battleships during the war. In the North Sea off Jutland on 31 May–1 June 1916, the German fleet, commanded by Vice Admiral Reinhard Scheer, squared off against the Royal Navy, led by Admiral Sir John Jellicoe. The engagement was a stand-off, as the Germans, outmanoeuvred by the larger British fleet, managed to escape and inflicted more damage on the British fleet than they received. Strategically, however, the British asserted their control of the sea, and most of the German surface fleet were confined to port for the rest of the war.

"Anyone who has ever looked into the glazed eyes of a soldier dying on the battlefield will think hard before starting a war."

Otto von Bismarck

U-boats tried to cut the supply lines between North America and Britain. The nature of submarine warfare meant that attacks often came without warning, giving the crews of the merchant ships little hope of survival. The US protested, and Germany changed its rules of engagement. After the sinking of the passenger liner *Lusitania* in 1915, Germany promised not to destroy passenger liners, while Britain armed its merchant ships, placing them beyond the protection of the "cruiser rules", which demanded warning and placing crews in "a place of safety" (a standard that lifeboats did not meet). Finally, in early 1917, Germany adopted a policy of unrestricted submarine warfare, realising that the Americans would eventually enter the war. Germany sought to strangle Allied sea lanes before the US could transport a large army overseas, but could maintain only five long-range U-boats on station, to limited effect.

The U-boat threat lessened in 1917, when merchant ships began travelling in convoys, escorted by destroyers. This made it difficult for U-boats to find targets, which lessened losses. After the hydrophone and depth charges were introduced, accompanying destroyers attacked submerged submarines with some hope of success. Convoys slowed the flow of supplies, since ships had to wait as they were assembled. The solution was an extensive program of building new freighters. Troopships were too fast for the submarines and did not travel the North Atlantic in convoys. The U-boats sank more than 5000 Allied ships, at a cost of 199 submarines.

# The war in the air

It was 1912 when aviation design genius Igor Sikorsky started work on the Ilya Muromets, a four-engine airliner that was quickly converted to a bomber during the war. It first flew on 10 December 1913. It was a mere 10 years since the Wright brothers had lifted off the beach at Kitty Hawk in the first powered and controlled heavier-than-air machine, yet here was a four-engine monster that could carry – and drop – 500kg of bombs.

Across the Channel seven months later the launch of the Vickers FB5 at Brooklands, Surrey, on 17 July 1914, marked the start of aerial combat. The FB – Fighting Biplane – was appropriately nicknamed the Gun Bus.

One of those the FB5 harried was launched on 23 May 1915 – the German Empire's Fokker Eindecker, the first aircraft that allowed the pilot to fire a machinegun through the arc of the propeller without hitting the blades.

Aircraft carriers were used for the first time, with HMS *Furious* launching Sopwith Camels in a raid to destroy the Zeppelin hangars at Tondern in 1918.

Manned observation balloons, floating high above the trenches, were used as stationary reconnaissance platforms, reporting enemy movements and directing artillery. Balloons commonly had a crew of two, equipped with parachutes, so that if there was an air attack they could bale out safely.

# All blood runs red.

Phrase painted on the side
of the plane flown by
Eugene Bullard,
the first black combatant

# 1917

The British naval blockade began to have a serious effect on Germany in 1917. In response, the German General Staff persuaded Chancellor Theobald von Bethmann-Hollweg to declare unrestricted submarine warfare, aimed at starving Britain out. German planners estimated that unrestricted submarine warfare would cost Britain a monthly shipping loss of 600,000 tonnes. The General Staff acknowledged that the policy would almost certainly bring the United States into the conflict, but calculated that British shipping losses would be so high that they would be forced to sue for peace after five or six months, before American intervention could take effect. In reality, tonnage sunk rose above 500,000 tonnes a month from February to July. It peaked at 860,000 in April. After July, the reintroduced convoy system became extremely effective in reducing the U-boat threat. Britain was safe from starvation, while German industrial output fell and US troops joined the war in large numbers far earlier than Germany had expected.

On 3 May 1917, during the Nivelle offensive, the weary French 2nd Colonial Division, veterans of the Battle of

Verdun, refused their orders, arriving drunk and without their weapons. Their officers could not punish an entire division, and harsh measures were not immediately implemented. But the mutiny affected another 54 French divisions and saw 20,000 men desert. However, appeals to patriotism and duty, as well as mass arrests and trials, encouraged the soldiers to return to defend their trenches, although they refused to take part in further offensive action.

The victory of the Central Powers at the Battle of Caporetto led the Allies to convene the Rapallo Conference, at which they formed the Supreme War Council to co-ordinate planning. Previously, British and French armies had operated under separate commands.

In December, the Central Powers signed an armistice with Russia. This released large numbers of German troops for use in the west. With German reinforcements and new American troops pouring in, the outcome was to be decided on the Western Front.

Emperor Charles I of Austria secretly tried separate peace negotiations with Clemenceau, with his wife's brother Sixtus in Belgium as an intermediary, without the knowledge of Germany. Italy opposed the proposals. When the negotiations failed, the attempt was revealed to Germany, resulting in a diplomatic catastrophe.

# Entry of the United States

"There is a price which is too great to pay for peace, and that price can be put in one word. One cannot pay the price of self-respect."

Woodrow Wilson

The United States pursued a policy of non-intervention at the start of the war, avoiding conflict while trying to broker a peace. When a German U-boat sank the British liner *Lusitania* on 7 May 1915 with 128 Americans among the dead, President Woodrow Wilson insisted that "America is too proud to fight", but demanded an end to attacks on passenger ships. Germany complied. Wilson unsuccessfully tried to mediate a settlement, but he also repeatedly warned that the US would not tolerate unrestricted submarine warfare, in violation of international law. Former president Theodore Roosevelt denounced German acts as "piracy". Wilson was narrowly re-elected in 1916 as his supporters emphasised "he kept us out of war".

Germany invited Mexico to join the war as its ally against the US. In return, the Germans would finance Mexico's war and help it recover Texas, New Mexico and Arizona. Britain intercepted the message and gave it to the US embassy in London. President Wilson made the note public, and Americans saw it as a cause for war. After the sinking of seven US merchant ships by submarines and the publication of the Mexico telegram, Wilson called for war on Germany, which the US Congress declared on 6 April 1917.

The US was never formally a member of the Allies, but became a self-styled "associated power". It had a small army, but after the passage of the Selective Service Act it drafted 2.8 million men and, by the summer of 1918, was sending 10,000 fresh soldiers to France every day. Germany had miscalculated, believing it would be months before American soldiers would arrive and that their arrival could be stopped by U-boats.

The US Navy sent a battleship group to Scapa Flow to join the British Grand Fleet, destroyers to Ireland and submarines to help guard convoys. Marines were also sent to France. The British and French wanted American units to reinforce their troops on the battle lines and not waste scarce shipping on bringing over supplies.

Spring Offensive
of 1918

General Erich Ludendorff drew up plans for the 1918 offensive on the Western Front, which sought to divide the British and French with feints and advances. The German leadership hoped to end the war before significant US forces arrived. The operation started on 21 March 1918, with an attack on British forces near Amiens. The Germans advanced an unprecedented 60km.

British and French trenches were penetrated using novel infiltration tactics. Previous attacks had featured long artillery bombardments and massed assaults. However, in the Spring Offensive of 1918, Ludendorff used artillery only briefly and infiltrated small groups of infantry at weak points. They attacked command and logistics areas and bypassed points of serious resistance. More heavily armed infantry then destroyed these positions. German success relied on surprise.

The front moved to within 120km of Paris. Three Krupp railway guns fired 183 shells on the capital, causing many Parisians to flee. The offensive was so successful that the Kaiser declared 24 March a national holiday. Many Germans thought victory was near. After heavy fighting, however, the offensive was halted. Lacking tanks or motorised artillery, the Germans were unable to consolidate their gains. This was not helped by the supply lines now being stretched because of their rapid advance. Arriving American troops were assigned to the depleted French and British Empire commands on 28 March. A Supreme War Council of Allied forces was created on 5 November 1917. General Ferdinand Foch was appointed supreme commander of the Allied forces. Haig, Petain and Pershing retained tactical control of their armies. Foch assumed a coordinating rather than a directing role, and the British, French and US commands operated largely independently.

By 20 July, the Germans were back across the Marne at their starting lines, having achieved little. After this last phase of the war in the West, the German Army never regained the initiative. German casualties between March and April 1918 were 270,000, including many storm troopers.

Meanwhile, Germany was falling apart at home. Anti-war marches became frequent and morale in the army fell. Industrial output was 53 per cent of 1913 levels.

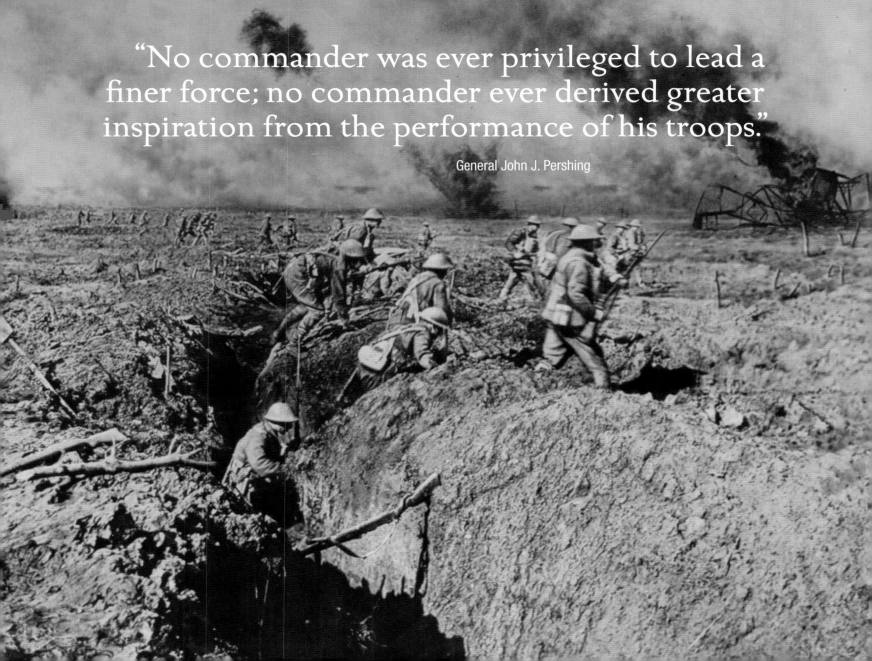

"No commander was ever privileged to lead a finer force; no commander ever derived greater inspiration from the performance of his troops."

General John J. Pershing

# Hundred Days Offensive

The Allied counteroffensive, known as the Hundred Days Offensive, began on 8 August 1918, with the Battle of Amiens, which involved more than 400 tanks and 120,000 British, Dominion, and French troops. By the end of the first day a gap of 24km had been created in the German lines. The defenders' morale collapsed, causing Ludendorff to call this day the "Black Day of the German army". After an advance as far as 23km, German resistance stiffened, and the battle ended on 12 August.

Rather than continuing the Amiens battle, the Allies shifted their attention. Allied leaders had now realised that to continue an attack after resistance had hardened was a waste of lives, and it was better to turn a line than to try to roll over it. They began quick attacks to take advantage of successful advances on the flanks, then broke them off when each attack lost its impetus.

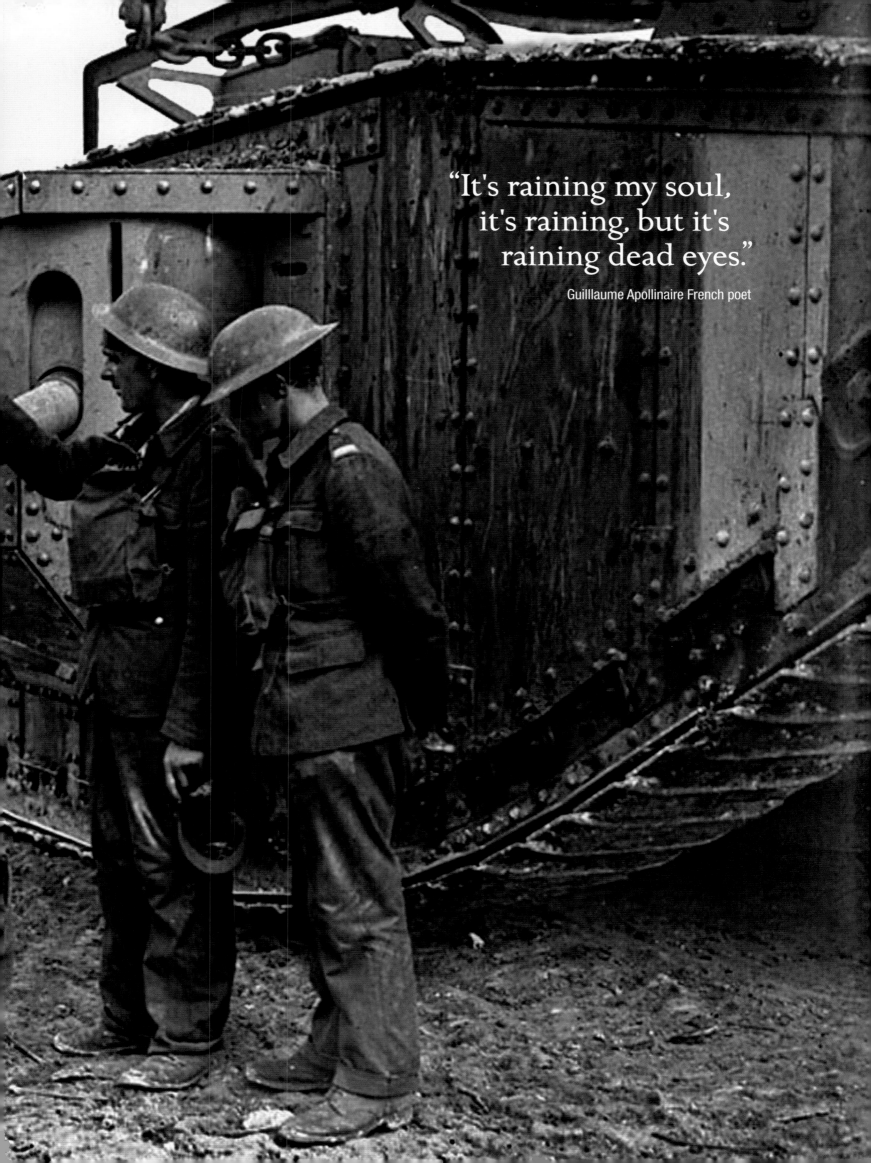

"It's raining my soul,
it's raining, but it's
raining dead eyes."

Guilllaume Apollinaire French poet

British, Dominion and smaller attached US forces launched the next phase with the Battle of Albert on 21 August, which marked the beginning of the Second Battle of the Somme. The assault was widened by French and then further British forces in the following days. During the last week of August the pressure along a 110km front against the enemy was heavy and unrelenting. From German accounts, "Each day was spent in bloody fighting against an ever and again on-storming enemy, and nights passed without sleep in retirements to new lines."

Faced with these advances, on 2 September the German Supreme Army Command issued orders to withdraw to the Hindenburg Line in the south. This ceded without a fight the salient seized the previous April. According to Ludendorff, "We had to admit the necessity ...to withdraw the entire front from the Scarpe to the Vesle."

September saw the Allies advance to the Hindenburg Line in the north and centre. The Germans continued to fight strong rearguard actions and launched counterattacks on lost positions, but only a few succeeded, and then only temporarily. Contested towns, villages, heights and trenches in the outposts of the Hindenburg Line continued to fall to the Allies, with the BEF alone taking 30,441 prisoners in the last week of September. On 24 September an assault by both the British and French came within 3km of St Quentin. The Germans were now completely back in the Hindenburg Line.

In nearly four weeks of fighting from 8 August, more than 100,000 German prisoners were taken, 75,000 by the BEF and the rest by the French. The German High Command realised the war was lost and tried to reach a satisfactory end. The day after that battle, Ludendorff said: "We cannot win the war any more, but we must not lose it either." On 11 August he offered his resignation to the Kaiser, who refused it, replying, "I see that we must strike a balance. We have nearly reached the limit of our powers of resistance. The war must be ended." On 13 August, at Spa, Hindenburg, Ludendorff, the Chancellor and Foreign Minister Hintz agreed that the war could not be ended militarily. Austria and Hungary warned that they could continue the war only until December, and Ludendorff recommended immediate peace negotiations.

On 10 September Hindenburg urged peace moves to Emperor Charles of Austria, and Germany appealed to the Netherlands for mediation. On 14 September Austria sent a note to all belligerents and neutrals suggesting a meeting for peace talks on neutral soil, and on 15 September Germany made a peace offer to Belgium. Both peace offers were rejected, and on 24 September the German Supreme Army Command told the leaders in Berlin that armistice talks were inevitable.

The final assault on the Hindenburg Line was launched by French and American troops on 26 September. The next week, French and American units broke through in Champagne at the Battle of Blanc Mont Ridge, forcing the Germans off the commanding heights, and closing towards the Belgian frontier. On 8 October the line was pierced again by British and Dominion troops at the Battle of Cambrai. The

German army had to shorten its front and use the Dutch frontier as an anchor to fight rearguard actions as it fell back towards Germany.

News of Germany's impending defeat spread through the German armed forces. The threat of mutiny was rife. Admiral Reinhard Scheer and Ludendorff decided to launch a last attempt to restore the "valour" of the German Navy. Knowing the government of Prince Maximilian of Baden would veto any such action, Ludendorff decided not to tell him. Nonetheless, word of the impending assault reached sailors at Kiel. Many, refusing to be part of a naval offensive they believed to be suicidal, rebelled and were arrested. Ludendorff took the blame. The Kaiser dismissed him on 26 October.

The collapse of the Balkans meant that Germany was about to lose its main supplies of oil and food. Its reserves had been used. The Americans supplied more than 80 per cent of Allied oil during the war, meaning no such loss of supplies could affect the Allied effort.

Having suffered over 6 million casualties, Germany moved towards peace. Prince Maximilian of Baden took charge of a new government as Chancellor of Germany to negotiate with the Allies. Telegraphic negotiations with President Wilson began immediately, in the vain hope that he would offer better terms than the British and French. Instead, Wilson demanded the abdication of the Kaiser. There was no resistance when the Social Democrat Philipp Scheidemann on 9 November declared Germany to be a republic. Imperial Germany was dead; a new Germany had been born: the Weimar Republic.

# The armistice

At 5am on 11 November 1918, an armistice with Germany was signed in a railway carriage at Compiègne. At 11am that day – the eleventh hour of the eleventh day of the eleventh month – a ceasefire came into effect. During the six hours between the signing of the armistice and its taking effect, opposing armies on the Western Front began to withdraw from their positions, but fighting continued along many areas of the front, as commanders wanted to capture territory before the war ended. Canadian Private George Lawrence Price was shot by a German sniper at 10.57 and died at 10.58. American Henry Gunther was killed 60 seconds before the armistice came into force while charging astonished German troops who were aware the Armistice was nearly upon them.

By November 1918, the Allies had ample supplies of men and equipment to invade Germany. Yet at the time of the armistice no Allied force had crossed the German frontier. The Western Front was still almost 1400km from Berlin and the Kaiser's armies had retreated from the battlefield in good order. These factors enabled Hindenburg and other senior German leaders to spread the story that their armies had not really been defeated. This resulted in the stab-in-the-back story, which attributed Germany's defeat not to its inability to continue fighting (even though up to a million soldiers were suffering from the 1918 flu pandemic and unfit to fight), but to the public's failure to respond to its "patriotic calling" and the supposed intentional sabotage of the war effort, particularly by Jews, Socialists, and Bolsheviks.

THE
# TREATY OF PEACE
BETWEEN
## THE ALLIED AND ASSOCIATED POWERS
AND
### GERMANY,
The Protocol annexed thereto, the Agreement respecting
the military occupation of the territories of the Rhine,
AND THE
## TREATY
BETWEEN
### FRANCE AND GREAT BRITAIN
RESPECTING
Assistance to France in the event of unprovoked
aggression by Germany.

Signed at Versailles, June 28th, 1919.

*(With Maps and Signatures in facsimile.)*

LONDON: PRINTED AND PUBLISHED BY HIS MAJESTY'S STATIONERY OFFICE.
To be purchased through any Bookseller or directly from H.M. STATIONERY OFFICE at the
following addresses: IMPERIAL HOUSE, KINGSWAY, LONDON, W.C.2; and 28, ABINGDON STREET,
LONDON, S.W.1; 37, PETER STREET, MANCHESTER; 1, ST. ANDREW'S CRESCENT, CARDIFF;
23, FORTH STREET, EDINBURGH; or from E. PONSONBY, LTD., 116, GRAFTON STREET, DUBLIN.

# Treaty of Versailles

A formal state of war between the two sides lasted another seven months, until the signing of the Treaty of Versailles with Germany on 28 June 1919. However, the American public opposed ratification of the treaty, mainly because of the League of Nations the treaty created. The US did not formally end its involvement in the war until the Knox–Porter Resolution was signed in 1921. After the Treaty of Versailles, treaties were signed with Austria, Hungary, Bulgaria and the Ottoman Empire. However, the negotiation of the treaty with the Ottoman Empire was followed by strife (the Turkish War of Independence), and a final peace treaty between the Allied Powers and the country that would become the Republic of Turkey was not signed until 24 July 1923, at Lausanne.

In signing the treaty, Germany acknowledged "all the loss and damage to which the Allied and associated governments and their nationals have been subjected as a consequence of the war imposed upon them by the aggression of Germany and her allies". This clause was also inserted in the treaties signed by the other members of the Central Powers. It became known, to Germans, as the War Guilt clause.

The treaties of the Paris conference also required the defeated powers to pay reparations. The Treaty of Versailles caused enormous bitterness in Germany, which nationalist movements exploited, especially the Nazis.

Runaway inflation in the 1920s contributed to the economic collapse of the Weimar Republic, and the payment of reparations was suspended in 1931 after the stock market crash of 1929 and the beginnings of the Great Depression worldwide.

Austria-Hungary was partitioned into several states, including Austria, Hungary, Czechoslovakia and Yugoslavia, largely along ethnic lines. Transylvania was shifted from Hungary to Greater Romania. The details were contained in the Treaty of Saint-Germain and the Treaty of Trianon. As a result of the Treaty of Trianon, 3.3 million Hungarians came under foreign rule. Although the Hungarians made up 54 per cent of the population of the pre-war Kingdom of Hungary, only 32 per cent of its territory was left to Hungary. Between 1920 and 1924, 354,000 Hungarians fled former Hungarian territories attached to Romania, Czechoslovakia and Yugoslavia.

The Russian Empire, which had withdrawn from the war in 1917 after the October Revolution, lost much of its western frontier as the newly independent nations of Estonia, Finland, Latvia, Lithuania, and Poland were carved from it.

The Ottoman Empire disintegrated, and much of its non-Anatolian territory was awarded to Allied powers as protectorates. The Turkish core was reorganised as the Republic of Turkey. The Ottoman Empire was to be partitioned by the Treaty of Sevres of 1920, but this treaty was never ratified by the Sultan and was rejected by the Turkish republican movement, leading to the Turkish Independence War and, ultimately, to the 1923 Treaty of Lausanne.

# War crimes

The "ethnic cleansing" of the Ottoman Empire's Armenian population, including mass deportations and executions, during the final years of the Ottoman Empire is considered genocide. The Ottomans saw the Armenian population as an enemy that had chosen to side with Russia at the beginning of the war. In early 1915, some Armenians joined the Russian forces, and the Ottoman government used this as a pretext to issue the Law on Deportation. This authorised the deportation of Armenians from the Empire's eastern provinces to Syria between 1915 and 1917. The exact number of deaths is unknown: the International Association of Genocide Scholars estimates over 1 million. The government of Turkey has consistently rejected charges of genocide, arguing that those who died were victims of inter-ethnic fighting, famine, or disease. Other ethnic groups were similarly attacked by the Ottoman Empire during this period, including Assyrians and Greeks, and some scholars consider those events to be part of the same policy of extermination.

Many pogroms accompanied the Russian Revolution of 1917 and the ensuing Russian Civil War; 60,000–200,000 civilian Jews were killed in the atrocities throughout the former Russian Empire.

German invaders treated any resistance – such as sabotaging railway lines – as illegal and immoral, and shot the offenders and burned buildings. They also tended to suspect that most civilians were potential guerrillas and took and sometimes killed hostages from among the civilian population. The German army executed over 6500 French and Belgian civilians between August and November 1914, usually in near-random large-scale shootings of civilians ordered by junior German officers. The German Army destroyed 15,000–20,000 buildings, including the university library at Louvain, and generated a wave of refugees of over a million people. Over half the German regiments in Belgium were involved in major incidents. Thousands of workers were shipped to Germany to work in factories.

"I used to see them there, marching back with a slow, dogged march, old men and young men with haggard looks, hardly any food. Going back to a place where their womenfolk is looking for the men that is dead, lying in the fields. It's a ghastly thing."

Australian Army Signaller Bill Harney

# Prisoners of war

About eight million men surrendered and were held in POW camps during the war. All nations pledged to follow the Hague Conventions on fair treatment of prisoners, and POWs' rate of survival was generally higher than that of men at the front.

Germany held 2.5 million prisoners, Russia 2-3 million and Britain and France about 720,000. Most were captured just before the Armistice. The most dangerous moment was the act of surrender, when helpless soldiers were sometimes gunned down. Once prisoners reached a camp, conditions were generally satisfactory (and much better than in World War II), thanks in part to the International Red Cross and inspections by neutral nations. However, conditions were terrible in Russia: starvation was common for prisoners and civilians. About 15–20 per cent of the prisoners in Russia died. In Germany, food was scarce, but only 5 per cent died.

The Ottoman Empire often treated POWs poorly. About 11,800 British Empire soldiers, most of them Indians, became prisoners after the Siege of Kut in Mesopotamia in April 1916. Although many were in bad condition when captured, Ottoman officers forced them to march 1100km to Anatolia. A survivor said: "We were driven along like beasts; to drop out was to die." The survivors were then forced to build a railway through the Taurus Mountains.

While the Allied prisoners of the Central Powers were quickly sent home, the same treatment was not granted to prisoners of the Allies and Russia, many of whom served as forced labour until 1920. They were released only after many approaches by the Red Cross to the Allied Supreme Council. German prisoners were still being held in Russia as late as 1924.

**YOUR KING & COUNTRY**

**NEED** YOU

ENLIST AT COLSTON HALL, BRISTOL.

**AT ONCE.**

THE FAMOUS
**13TH, 42ND AND 73RD**
**BATTALIONS C.E.F.**
ROYAL HIGHLANDERS OF CANADA
ALLIED WITH THE BLACK WATCH

Require Reinforcements

**250 MEN**

Will be sent Overseas immediately

Here is a chance for YOU to join Battalions
that have already won fame at the Front.

Apply at once to Armoury
**429 BLEURY STREET - - MONTREAL**

*Boys*
*Come over here*
*you're wanted*

Australia has promised Britain
**50,000** MORE MEN
WILL **YOU** HELP US KEEP THAT PROMISE

LANGEMARCK
ST. JULIEN
FESTUBERT
GIVENCHY

New names in
Canadian history.

More are coming—
Will you be there?

**ENLIST !**

Make us as proud of you
as we are of him !

*The* TRUMPET CALLS

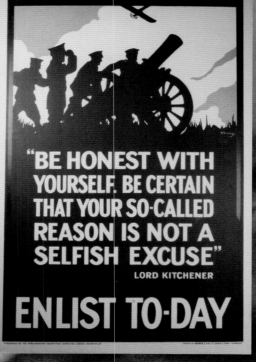

"BE HONEST WITH
YOURSELF. BE CERTAIN
THAT YOUR SO-CALLED
REASON IS NOT A
SELFISH EXCUSE"
LORD KITCHENER

**ENLIST TO-DAY**

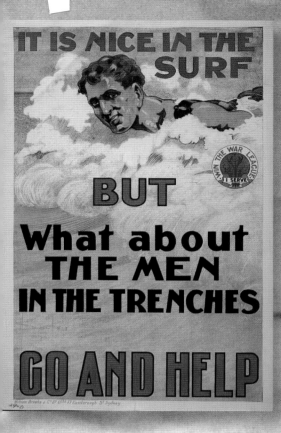

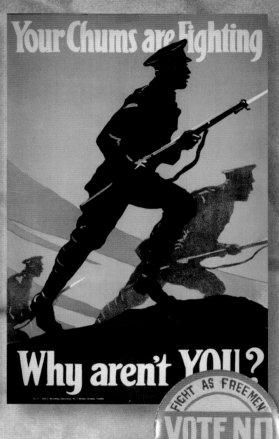

# Conscription

Canada's 1917 conscription crisis erupted when the Conservative Prime Minister, Robert Borden, brought in compulsory military service over the objection of French-speaking Quebecers. It opened a gap between French Canadians, who believed their loyalty should be to Canada and not to the British Empire, and members of the Anglophone majority, who saw the war as a duty to both Britain and Canada. Of 625,000 Canadians who served, 60,000 were killed and 173,000 wounded.

In Australia, a sustained pro-conscription campaign by Prime Minister Billy Hughes caused a split in the Australian Labor Party, so Hughes formed the Nationalist Party of Australia in 1917. Nevertheless, the labour movement, the Catholic Church and Irish nationalist expatriates successfully opposed Hughes' push, which was rejected in two plebiscites.

In Britain, conscription resulted in the calling up of nearly every physically fit man in Britain – six million of 10 million eligible. Of these, about 750,000 lost their lives and 1,700,000 were wounded. Most deaths were young unmarried men, but 160,000 had families.

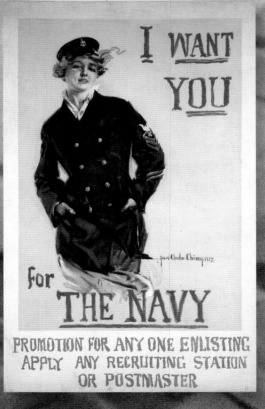

# An extraordinary day
## 23 August 1914

## Maurice Dease VC

A single company of Royal Fusiliers and a machinegun section with Lieutenant Maurice Dease in command were defending Nimy Bridge at Mons, Belgium. The gunfire was intense, and the casualties heavy – all his men were shot – but Dease kept firing despite his wounds, until he was hit for the fifth time and was carried away. He died of his wounds. Dease won the first Victoria Cross to be awarded in the war. He also won it on the first day of the first significant British encounter.

## Sidney Godley VC

When Dease had been mortally wounded and carried away, Private Godley held the bridge single-handed under heavy fire and was wounded twice. Shrapnel entered his back when an explosion near him went off, and he was shot in the head. Despite his injuries he carried on the defence of the bridge while his comrades escaped.

Godley defended the bridge for two hours, until he ran out of ammunition. He dismantled the gun and threw the pieces into the canal. He tried to crawl to safety, but advancing German soldiers caught him and took him to a prisoner of war camp. He died in England in 1957.

## Theodore Wright VC

On the same day at Mons, Captain Theodore Wright, 31, Corps of Royal Engineers, tried under heavy fire to connect a lead to demolish a bridge, and although wounded in the head, made a second attempt. At Vailly, France, on 14 September he helped the passage of the 5th Cavalry Brigade over a pontoon bridge and was hit while helping a wounded man into shelter. He died of his wounds.

## Charles Garforth VC

On the same day at Harmingnies, France, about 10km from Mons, Corporal Charles Garforth volunteered to cut wire under fire, which enabled his squadron to escape. On 2 September, under constant fire, he extricated a sergeant who was trapped under his dead horse, and carried him to safety. The next day, when another sergeant had lost his horse in a similar way, Garforth drew off the enemy fire and enabled the sergeant to get away. He spent the rest of the war as a prisoner, and died in England in 1973, aged 81.

# Most decorated

## Will Barker VC, DSO & bar, MC & two bars

Sunday, 27 October 1918. Canadian-born Royal Flying Corps pilot Will Barker is on a routine flight in his Sopwith Snipe in France to return it to the depot. Over the Marmal Forest he encounters a German Rumpler two-seater. Its skilful pilot and observer/gunner keep him at bay, and the gunner hits the Snipe. Eventually Barker circles away and, relying on his accurate gunnery, fires from 200 metres, killing the gunner. He quickly scores more hits on the vulnerable Rumpler, breaking it up in the air.

But in focusing on his victim he misses a Fokker behind him. Its gunfire smashes into his right leg. Although badly injured, Barker gets into a circling contest, which ends when his bullets hit the Fokker's fuel tank, setting it on fire.

Then Barker finds himself in the middle of a flight of Fokker and Albatros biplanes patrolling at high altitude. Spandau guns open up from every direction and another bullet smashes into his left leg. Somehow, he manages to shoot down two of these opponents before he faints and goes into a diving spin. The rush of air revives him and he comes to, still in the middle of German fighters. As they fire at him he selects

one and flies right at it, guns blazing. As they close, he blows it apart, then realises his left elbow has been hit.

Virtually crippled, with three limbs shattered, he passes out again. For a second time, he comes to in the middle of enemy aircraft, now quite low. Incredibly, he dispatches another. As he struggles to reach the safety of the British lines, a German bullet strikes his fuel tank, but it doesn't catch fire and Barker switches to reserve. Seconds later the Snipe crash-lands, skidding sideways and flipping over. The men of a Scottish infantry regiment who have watched his epic aerial battle pull him from the wreckage.

Barker has downed four enemy planes, taken several bullets, and survived to be awarded the Victoria Cross. He lies unconscious in hospital in Rouen for two weeks. He receives telegrams from King George V, the Prince of Wales, fellow ace Billy Bishop, and many others. Only his constitution pulls him through, but he is partially crippled for the rest of his life. He dies in 1930 at the age of 35. He is the most decorated war hero in the history of the British Commonwealth – VC, DSO and bar, MC and two bars, Mentioned in Despatches three times, Croix de Guerre and two Silver Medals of Military Valour (Italy).

# The Aces

## The United States

On 29 April 1918, Eddie Rickenbacker shot down his first plane. On 28 May he claimed his fifth to become an ace. On May 30, he scored his sixth victory. It was his last for 3½ months. He developed an ear infection in July which almost ended his flying career and grounded him for several weeks. He shot down Germany's hottest new fighter, the Fokker D.VII, on 14 September and another next day.

On 25 September, now a captain, he claimed two more German planes, for which he was belatedly awarded the Medal of Honor in 1931 by President Herbert Hoover. After claiming yet another Fokker D.VII on 27 September, he became a balloon buster by downing observation balloons on 28 September, 1 October, 27 October and 30 October.

Thirteen more wins followed in October, bringing his total to 13 Fokker D.VIIs, four other German fighters, five highly defended observation balloons, and only four easy two-seater reconnaissance planes.

Rickenbacker's 26 victories remained the American record until World War II. They were all achieved in only six months.